COUNTRY

TO

CORPORATE

Marissa Bright

Dedication

Thank you to my family and friends growing up in South Carolina.

You made my young life full of adventure.
Never forget who you are, where you come from and your Creator.
God is alive in you, and he is not limited to your location.

Special thanks to my mother and father, Mr. & Mrs. Bright.
You are my everything!

Grandparents, your sacrifice and hard work is not in vain.

Siblings, thank you for putting up with me, and pouring into me.

Myles, my precious son, this is just the beginning.

Ooh-wee, the gravel is hot today as I run barefooted on the newly laid asphalt. It may not be the best idea, but it feels so right to not have my toes locked in those shining jelly sandals that my mother deemed as cute. As I feel the breeze blow through my curls, I looked up to see the clouds as they race in the sky. Blue then gray, blue then gray. I wondered which cloud would win as I ran keeping my head up to mark my place. In the passerby I see the birds doing their thing. I see the trees dancing cheering on the competitors. The bees and bugs dance and sing near my ear, and then I hear my mother voice, slice and dice my concentration. "Get back in this yard and where are your shoes?!" I shrugged and ran back into the yard between the Crape Myrtle trees that lined the driveway so cleaver. Look at that entrance, my entrance to my royal palace. I began to spin and spin until the dizziness took over. Kaboom, into the grass I fell, and into the grass I laid. Again, the clouds caught my eye, and now I see that they are not moving at all. It is I that is running a race. It is me that is moving along the way.

During my childhood in the country, it was nothing for me to walk outside and get lost in the beauty of God's creation. The bugs, the birds, the sky and the signs were beautifully synced. Time in this world under the clouds has revealed to me the wisdom hidden deeply into the lessons of everyday life, that was taught by people who loved and cared for me. They knew, and often stated, "Just keep living". Just keep living, and it will all make sense, it will all come together.

In my young adult life, I quickly moved from the country living to corporate navigation, finding my way in an organization with many rules, politics and secret codes. I never imagined that playing in the mud, running for a school bus, and loving a dog would help me respond and conduct myself accordingly in a manner of dignity. I have experienced many setbacks and hurt by not allowing my experiences to permeate and dictate how I enter the workplace with confidence in who I am, who's I am, and what I know. Growing up, there were many preconceived notions about 'country folk'. We were not as smart, not as rich, and did not have as many resources as 'city folk'. Believing that prejudice subconsciously made me feel as I did not have a place, a voice, or a chance to go as far as I did. What changed? I asked Yeshua to give me knowledge of who I am and to reveal strategy to me of what would you have of me in the corporate setting?

Slowly, but surely, I started to slow down. The breeze started to catch my curls on my lunch breaks as I took a walk to think. The clouds began to race, and I was reminded that I needed to be still so I can realize I am moving onward. The birds began to dance in front of me, before taking flight in a new direction. I began to walk barefooted to feel the heat below my feet and it made me feel alive again. I want to reveal some childhood lessons that I learned and how it transferred to me operating in corporate settings. Grab a highlighter, lets travel from country to corporate.

What Is the End of a Cul-de-Sac?

I grew up in a small community with ranch and bungalow styled homes on a street that ended with a cul-de-sac. Community kickball and basketball games were the highlight of the weekend on Sunday after church and before dinner. The community included younger families with school aged kids, to retired families with grandchildren visiting over the summer. With birds chirping in the distance, I can hear my mother chatting on the phone with the other youth ministers. It sounds like it is going to be a full week production with the scheduled practices for the community parade. Although I know she is going to ask me to get up and make the bed, I lie there a little longer. I can smell the cleaning supplies marinating in the sinks and toilets. I can hear the washing machine dancing on the cemented floors on the porch. I shift in my bed when I notice the sheet is extra warm beneath me. Oh no! I did it again. I wet the bed. I jump up to get a head start stripping the bed before my mother comes in to give me that disappointed look. Sigh. I can't help it—the dreams seemed so real!

Sliding my feet from the side of the bed, I hear my sister aggressively yell, "Are you serious, Marissa?! You have to start waking up!"

"What is going on in there?" Mommy yells.

"Marissa peed the bed. Again!"

"Marissa! Take your butt in the tub!"

Bowing my head in shame, I slowly twist my lip up at my sister. What did she expect from me? I mean, I understand she is getting wet, too, but it is what happens when you sleep in a bunk bed. As my paternal grandmother (whom I call my Little Lady) would say, "Que Sera, Sera."

I go into the bathroom and begin to run the water, and as I look up, I get excited. It is Saturday! I jump inside the tub to open the window with the white frame, slightly above my head. To get leverage, I place one foot on the opposite side of the tub and one foot on the soap holder. I unlock and lift the window. Immediately I can smell the gardenia bush perfume dancing in the breeze. I can also hear the conversations carrying on outside and the whine of the lawn mower as my brother cuts the grass.

I finish bathing, come out dressed in my hand-me-down best and brush my teeth. I walk past my bedroom to see my mother finish stripping the bed; the mattress is missing. That poor mattress. As I walk to throw my clothes in the hamper on the porch—yes, our laundry room is outside—I see and smell breakfast. Breakfast is by far my mother's best meal. There are grits or French toast as the main carb, partnered with eggs, Roger Wood sausage, or fried bologna. Excited to eat with that thick Oh! Boy Syrup, I run off to complete my chores. I have to at least have my room cleaned before I can eat. Since most of my room is presently in the wash or airing out on the clothes-line, all I must do is vacuum.

Imagine sharing a small room with two sisters. We make it happen, with many life lessons thrown in. Being the youngest, I am given the hand-me-down clothes my older sisters no longer need.

While eating breakfast, there is a lot going on around me. Dad is down the street at the shop building cabinets or finishing a project that he did not complete the night before. The wind is blowing through the clothesline, the fresh breeze stirring up a smell of bleach and fabric softener. My sisters are discussing plans to get me in trouble, and my brother is still cutting the grass—likely complaining about it as he does.

After completing the chores, it is time to socialize and play! It's bike time. There are only two bikes, and three girls. If I plan the day right, my oldest sister will go cook with my Little Lady and my mid-sis will go into adventure land with me. Our adventures could be anything from climbing trees, fishing in the pond, hide-and-go-seek, picking grapes, or just swinging on the swing set.

Flying high and free is the name of the game. It drives my mother crazy. We swing so high. This is not one of the wooden planted swings. We use a simple aluminum swing from the community store. Man! We rock the swing front to back, front to back. Higher, higher, and then JUMP! I win! Finally. I beat my muscular built, but athletically uninterested sister who is shaped like a gymnast.

I remember one summer, we rocked the swing so high, it tilted over. No matter how much we tried to pick that swing up, we were unsuccessful. I remember it being a fun day until that moment. As we attempted to right our wrong, we heard my father's truck slowly come into the yard. He was coming home from a long day of work. It was hot, he was underpaid and overqualified. He'd been working in the sun all day only to drive home and find an aluminum swing on its side. The look on his face said it all. Concern, disappointment, exhaustion. Okay, maybe it was not that bad of a day, but that feeling of not being able to add a smile to his face when he came home to his sanctuary felt like fire in my chest.

After he and my brother picked the swing set back up, we placed cement blocks around the ankles of the set. Back to flying we went! Now, if we stayed anchored and our intent was pure, no one could stop us from flying high; no one could stop us from being free. Being free was the name of the game. After we got tired of being on the swing sets, we would ride our bikes until the sun began to set. Living on a street that ended in a cul-de-sac had its advantages. One, there was no exit on the end, so my mother felt safe letting us go because she would stay in the yard to see cars coming and going in the neighborhood. Two, there was a basketball goal at the end of the road, so the older kids of the neighborhood would play and not have to worry about passing traffic, the ball rolling in the road, or any newer people looking for a pick-up game. There was community. We would play and play until it was time to go home. There were many lessons learned in that small community that ended in a cul-de-sac. Little did I know, there is no end to a cul-de-sac.

When We Left Her Behind

I come from a family of hard workers. Unbeknownst to him, my father began his career around the age of four. He started learning the trade of carpentry and mathematics. He began to understand key concepts at an early age and became my grandfather's right hand in the construction business. As his family grew, and his ambitions were limited by his father's traditions, he decided to take a step in the direction of beginning his own construction company.

Young, ambitious, a father and a husband, my father was and is bold and consistent. There is only one night that I recall seeing my father stay in bed later than four in the morning on a weekday, and that is when I was sick and wanted to stay with him. Other than that, he would be up and moving, no matter if it was ninety degrees outside or twenty-five. I can still hear his truck warming up while he prepared his salted oats, toast, and black coffee in the kitchen. He never failed to leave enough for his wife and children. When I saw his spoon on the sink's edge from stirring his Maxwell instant coffee, I knew it was going to be a good day for him. He was a man of routine and when there were traces of his routine, I knew that all was well with him, my father that started his day before I finished my dreams. Because of those early departures and late returns, I would not get to see my father as much as I wanted to. But when he came back home every evening with exhaustion in his brown eyes, and that pretty smile, I knew it was all worth it. Whatever it was, he'd accomplished his daily mission.

Running a business was no joke and nothing to take lightly as a young black male in the South. What kept our family financially stable in the early years was my mother working as a nurse and paying tithes. Although my father jokes that she was fired up to five times, and she adamantly denies this, she was the woman with the long hair and white scrubs in my memory bank. There was no one purer and more caring than my mother. Yes, she was a drill sergeant, and now that I am a mother of my own, I get it. She was also a champion of the change she wanted to see.

To put this in perspective, my mother and father were married at the early age(s) of eighteen and twenty, respectively. By the tender ages of twenty-four and twenty-six, my mother and father had welcomed four children in this world. When my father decided to take the step to begin his dream of having the independence of his own company, my mother knew that for the ship to turn, it needed a steady stream. At thirty years young, she became that stream for her family of six.

The only time I recall my mother not dressing in her scrubs was when she was fulfilling her calling as a youth minister or when there was a special occasion. Anytime you would see my mother working, she would have on her crisp scrubs, lightly scented perfume, and her long hair curled down her back. She would either work the late shift at the nursing home or work the early shift as a dialysis nurse. Wherever she was, she did not complain. She knew that she had a family to take care of, and a husband striving for something better.

When you are running a business, it is hard to take days off. My father's skillset was, and still to this day is, unmatched. His attention to detail and passion for wood crafting is impeccable. His kryptonite? Administrative duties. Oh, I knew when he had to do paperwork—there was more coffee, fewer smiles, and less conversation. There was nothing I could do to help except give him hugs and kisses.

One day, I felt it worked! Now, as an adult, I can see that this was all planned in advance. But does that matter? No. This is my vantage point from a child's perspective. My father planned to take us to an arcade because I hugged him and took all the stress away. Could you imagine my excitement? I began to get dressed and so did my sisters. I have no clue where my brother was; that is a consistent theme in my childhood. As we were preparing to take our forty-minute trip to the arcade, I heard gospel music and smelled cleaning supplies coming from the kitchen. Mommy was home!

As I ran to greet her, she was sweeping the floor. She had on her scrubs, so I knew she still smelled sweet. I ran to give her a hug and told her that she needed to get dressed to go to the arcade. She looked at me and said that she could not go because she was only home on a short break. She'd never done this before, and I looked at her and said that she must go. The whole family was going, and I did not want to leave her behind. She looked at me and insisted that she would be fine and that she wanted me to behave myself and stay close to my father.

I was crushed. Not because I didn't get my way, but because I realized she was crushed to be left behind. She felt we would be having fun without her. I knew she felt that she would never get a break. I cried when we left, and even though it was fun, I wished my mother was there.

When we returned home, my mother was in the kitchen cooking dinner. When she heard us coming in the door, she turned around and smiled and said, "Well?"

I showed her the things I'd won, and for a second, I forgot that we had to leave her behind. I was so engaged in showing her my prizes. She was proud of me, and I saw her smile at my dad, which always made my day. When you have two hardworking parents, sometimes the most rewarding thing is to see them enjoy each other's company, versus bickering about who left the peanut butter jar half opened. This still happens today, and I think it is my mom.

Constant examples of hard work and consistency filled my childhood. My parents' faith and sacrificial lifestyle paid off. At the age of thirty-five, my father was able to build his wife the home that God had shown her in a dream as a young child. The house was large enough for his children to have space to grow and him to have an office. The best part of the building process for me was helping my father pour the foundation for the home. Seeing the framework, plumbing, and then pouring the cement was an exciting thing to watch and a fun way to spend time with my father.

In my career, as a young woman and mother, I have made sacrifices—from leaving my son with my parents for half a year to complete an internship in hopes of securing financial stability for us, to moving several states away to grab the opportunity for a promotion. I have seen many buses leave to go to arcades without me. There were times I wanted to stop and be young and dumb, but I could not. There was something in me that I could not quiet, could not ignore. I saw the frame and the foundation; I saw the weather beams installed to prepare the walls for the storm. I saw the blood and the bandages during installation. I saw the step-by-step process and I helped pour the cement. I knew what it took to succeed, and I knew that I could not get distracted.

Transferrable Lessons

1. Spoon dripping in coffee: In this world, change is inevitable and encouraged. One thing that you may not have considered is finding your voice and your routine. To become successful, you need to be able to identify what makes you stand apart, create a plan and routine, and perfect it. You may tweak it, build on it, and use it in different arenas. Ultimately, that thing is what others will depend on. Remain consistent and dependable. Find that thing that makes you stand apart and keep shining!

2. Behave yourself and stay close to your Father: Outside triggers and circumstances will cause you to react. How will you react when you are falsely blamed for matters that were above you? How will you react when the credit for your hard work is given to another manager? How will you respond when your integrity is tested? There are many things that I did not foresee coming my way in a cubicle. But one thing is for sure: I continue to behave myself and stay close to my Father. Prayer and meditation are the keys to success when you are facing the storm. Learning how to find inner peace will prevent you from being a tyrant. When all is against you, and you think, "What now?!" and you want to throw in the towel, remember the story of Joseph. He was sold by his brothers

into slavery because of jealousy. He was then falsely accused and thrown into jail. While in jail, at his lowest point, he was able to live with purpose and display the gift that no one knew or saw he possessed—a gift that was ultimately discovered by a pharaoh, the highest official at the time. Never do you hear about Joseph complaining; never do you hear about him losing faith. Joseph remained consistent even in times when he felt forgotten, and he was lifted above the nations. He was able to use his gift of administration to save the Nation of Egypt. I imagine every trial in his life, his character and gift were being molded to prepare him for his purpose, which was grand! He was set apart by being open for God to use him as a vessel to interpret the dreams of a Pharoah which opened the door for other things to come. In your season of hardship, "behave" yourself and stay close to your Father Yeshua. Everything will work out in your favor.

3. Perfume: As a child, I could not see my mother's exhaustion. I could not interpret fear or disbelief in her because, to me, she was always in her white scrubs and fragranced with sweet perfume. Many times, you may not feel like doing what you have been assigned to do in the workplace. You may feel like you have different gifts, or you may want to learn a different task, or be in front of a different audience. All valid feelings, and you should continue to position yourself for the things you desire. One thing my mother taught me without saying it is that you must be prepared for the audience and for the opportunity before you can see in the natural. What if my mother dressed the way she felt on days she lacked enthusiasm? What if you could look at her and be able to tell that this twenty-four-year-old with four kids, a husband, and a dog named Mudbone was in over her head? Any sane person would run the other way. But that was not the case. People were so drawn to her. Her sweet aroma welcomed broken hearts. Her pure presence drew in the hopeless parents. Her prayers were heard by the angels. My mother went through her tough times with grace, and because of her sweet perfume, I have seen God open doors for her that people with more "credentials" could not

pry open with a crowbar. Never look like your circumstance in the natural, and never let your circumstance kill you in the spirit. Instead, be of a sweet aroma wherever you go and allow your gift to make room for you.

4. Weather beams are a part of the foundation: Steel beams installed in skyscrapers are there to ensure that the building can move with the wind without breaking. When I "inspected" my father's installation of weather beams on his two-story brick home, I was surprised. What it showed me is that you don't have to be a skyscraper to experience shifts and storms. Furthermore, you shouldn't wait to be a skyscraper to prepare for them. Equip yourself with the necessary tools to withstand hardships in the workplace. I am southern, and I am a Christian. There is a myth that prayer solves all things. You should pray before blindly walking into situations, new opportunities, or the boardroom. Be inspired by Yeshua's way of life. He was constantly praying, but He followed many business practices that you may see today.

    a. Recruited: He recruited disciples to be fishers of men. Not only did He know their potential, but He also knew of their weaknesses. He did not recruit them and leave them to wander. He walked with them, and He talked with them, and He trained them of His kingdom's culture; how they should conduct themselves.

    b. Built His brand: When people spoke about Yeshua, they spoke about what He stood for. He was about love, order, and fulfilling divine purpose. He preached the gospel; He was the word. Love it or hate it, He did no waiver from His brand, and He was identifiable through actions.

    c. Saw it through: When Yeshua knew His journey on the earth was coming to an end, He sought his Father for more understanding. He had his Last Supper and He saw the purpose of His life to the end.

In the work environment, it is so easy to wonder: "What if they fire me? What if they don't need me anymore? What if they see that I am not qualified to handle this task?" I will tell you this. If your foundation in life was installed properly, you are more secure than you know. Sometimes, you don't realize how strong you are until the storm comes—and when it passes by you are still standing. This may not be the best thing to hear. If you do not feel that your foundation is strong, and you do not feel that you have what it takes, it is okay to be broken and start over.

Every day that you are here, there is a chance to get it right. At the job, it can feel as though you are in a different dimension, but that is an illusion. Every day that you spend there is a day that you will never get back. Every meeting that you are involved in, you are an influencer of the people who are under your voice. Every security guard you encounter, or cleaning professional that you walk past, are people just like you. Walk in light and sweet aromas. Fill the room with love and passion. Your drive, your consistency, your preparation, and your aroma will open doors for you that your degree, on its own, cannot! Be like Yeshua and handle your business. Be like my parents and be consistent.

On the Horse

Growing up in the country, it is a clever idea to have a best friend, whether that is a make-believe friend, an animal, or a human. In my neighborhood, there was a good age mixture of kids running around. We rarely had a quiet Saturday or evening when everyone stayed in the house. When the bus dropped off the older kids, and they did not have football practice, it was on. You would hear the basketball meeting the gravel at the "curb," which is the nickname for the cul-de-sac. Sometimes there would be bicycle races; other times, there would just be conversations with one foot on the petal and one foot on the street. On Saturdays, everyone would make their way to the "candy lady's house" down the street to get frozen ice pop, chips, or candy bars.

In the fall, on Saturday mornings, you would smell fire from the neighborhood dads, and sons burning leaves that fell from the trees. We would sometimes run and jump in the highest pile and watch the leaves go up like a big splash, scattering all around. We were also aware that, after we jumped, we had five seconds to get up and run from my oldest brother, who had been up since sunrise raking the leaves into piles.

In the neighborhood, I would watch as all the kids had friends their age that they would connect with. As the baby of my family, I attempted to get along with my older siblings' friends as best as possible, but I would always get the stare-down, the go-home, or the silent treatment. Especially when mid-sister, who was closest to me in age, decided to grow up, I was left to play with myself a lot. There was one kid in the neighborhood who always made my day, and always made me laugh. Growing up in the country, when you had a friend of the opposite sex, there was always a stigma that this person was your boyfriend, or girlfriend, and you were sitting in the tree, K-I-S-S-I-N-G. You know the drill. Well, I was an independent girl, and I did not have time to be tied down to a foolish boy, so I would always keep my distance. At least I attempted to. I would flirt with my brother's friends, who were ten years my senior. Some of them were even related to me. I didn't care, though. My heart was set on possibilities—until the event happened. My childhood adventures would never be the same.

When I was around the age of six, I was playing on the porch one day as my mother talked on the phone and swept. As she would talk, I would wonder off and play with insects and flowers. As long as she could see me, I would go on adventures in the yard. As I played in the yard, I heard a horse coming down the street. I looked up and saw this kid on a horse with nothing but his tighty-whities underwear on! He looked down at me and asked if I wanted to ride. As I looked up in amazement, I laughed my little chubby butt off. He held out his hand, and I attempted to jump on the horse. I have always been amazed by the strength and beauty of a horse. Well, after the third attempt, I made it and the horse took three steps. My mother's conversation grew stale, and she realized what I was up to. "Boy!!!" she yelled. "GO HOME and put on pants!!"

We both looked at each other when we realized she was serious. I bowed my head in amazement and hilarity of how upset my mother was, and I slid off the horse. I looked up at him and said, "Another day?" He tilted his head and rode off in the sunset. Well, not really, just down the road. I heard my mother call his mother and tell her my new best friend was down the road riding his horse naked. It tickled me pink. I tried to hold it in, but I could not.

After that day, my friend would come and knock on the door and ask if I wanted to play. We would ride our bikes to his house and to mine. He would often bring me chocolate clusters candies that I liked. I soon discovered those were his mother's as she chased him out the house while he had the chocolates in his hand. Laughing as if he did not have a care in the world, and unmoved by his mother's threats, he ran while yelling at me to run and jump on the bike. He was the dirtiest boy I knew, from all his farm chores, and the most understanding. We both had this habit of biting the inside of our cheeks, as if we had chewing tobacco. We would hold conversations for hours while he wet the hogs, moved hay, and run the chickens. Not once did he ever ask me to help him, but he was always eager to hear my stories and bring me chocolates.

Well, we grew older. We went from elementary school to high school and our friend circles grew. No matter who we were dating, what was going on in our lives, when we saw each other, we would ask how things were, and what was new. I went on to college, on a softball scholarship. Every weekend when I came home, and he would see my car in my parent's yard, he would wave at me while passing by on his tractor. Yes, I said it, he was still working on his tractor. If he caught my eye, I would sit on the porch, because I knew in about ten to fifteen minutes, he would return with his two-toned truck to chat.

I'll never forget the last time he stopped by to chat. We sat on the porch talking for hours about our love lives, work, and our parents. My dad happened to come home and catch us chatting. He waved at him and went in the house. My friend, in his one-piece work romper, stood up and said it was good seeing me and he had better get going and finish his work. I gave him a hug and he cranked up that truck, backed out of the yard, threw up his hat, put it back on his head, and drove off. Just like to good ol' days, when I went inside, my father was laughing and making jokes that he would tell my then "boyfriend" that I was outside talking on the porch with my one and only Brent. I smiled and shushed him off. Country folks always starting something.

I may have seen Brent one more time in passing before that day I was on the porch alone. This time, two years had passed, and I was expecting my son. Oh, how I needed someone to talk to, how I needed my friend. Instead, I sat there alone. It was a Sunday morning and I had just cooked breakfast when my Little Lady called. She asked me how I was doing, but I could hear in her voice that something was off. She then asked if I had spoken to anyone in the neighborhood. I hadn't—I'd just woken up. She told me to have a seat; she had some upsetting news. My best friend, who years ago had ridden a horse in his tighty-whities to express his interest in my friendship, had just gotten in a car accident the night before, only about a mile down the road. He had passed away. I could not speak; I could not eat. I could not even attend his funeral. Here I was, the summer before giving birth, and I was not strong enough to say goodbye. Instead, I stayed home, reflecting on all the good things, and what he meant to me and everyone with whom he had come in contact.

Still to this day, I cannot believe it has been a decade, and it hurts that I no longer see his tractor drive by. But there are things that I learned from my dear friend Brent and lessons that I apply to the workplace.

Transferable Lessons

1. Find your voice: In the workplace, depending on your company, there will be a pre-existing culture and certain behaviors that are expected of you. It is especially important to be able to adapt to your work environment, as well as to find your voice in your career. The easiest thing to do is to become the "yes man." Yes, I will stay late. Yes, I will work five years without a development plan or promotion. Yes, I will take on extra projects; just let me keep my job. The thing that God has shown me through my friend's southern roots, and deep country accent, is to be who you are. He was a hardworking young man, and his work ethic could not be denied. He treated everyone with kindness, although he loved a good debate. But one thing was for sure—everyone knew Brent's personality, his calm demeanor, his works, his smile. They knew his voice.

   In 1 Peter 4:10–11, it states that God has given each of you a gift from His great variety of spiritual gifts. Use them well to serve one another. Do you have a gift of speaking? Then speak as though God Himself were speaking through you. Do you have a gift of helping others? Do it with all the strength and energy that God supplies. Then everything you do will bring glory to God through Yeshua. All glory and power to Him forever and ever! Amen.

In corporations, if you are not careful, you will feel there is a singular line/ladder to success. Do this, say that, dress this way, and be mindful of who you offend. There is a code of conduct that must be followed in every situation, and it's important to be able to readily adapt. "Be strong and courageous. Do not be frightened, and do not be dismayed, for the lord your God is with you wherever you go" (Joshua 1:9). If you are living a life to honor God, and He opens a door for you, He will not leave you. He will be there by your side. There is a saying: "If He brought you to it, He will bring you through it."

God will not bring you to new things in your life and abandon you. He made you in His image. Find your voice in the workplace, in your life, and live abundantly. Don't settle for safe; don't settle for the singular ladder to success. We all have gifts, we all have passions, and we all have a horse and a voice. We all will have moments to ride up, exposed and transparent, just as we are, with the intent of making the biggest impact to whatever arena we enter. Be bold! Be courageous, consistent, and courteous. I can only hope that my friend Brent knew the impact he had on this country girl, who needed to be embraced by his presence to know—it is okay to be yourself. When you leave, there will never be another you. Don't live your life thinking about what-ifs, what now—just know it is okay to be free. God tells us to be courageous, be bold! You were made in His image. Find your voice, ask God to reveal your thing, and do it to the absolute best of your ability, bringing glory to your Maker's name.

2. Just get it done: One thing I did not reflect on too much as a kid is that my friend had a lot of responsibilities. He lived on a farm with big, stinky animals. Even while I would talk with him, and eat the chocolate clusters he stole for me, he would be working. One thing I noticed—he never complained. He knew that he had things to do, and he did them, with a clear understanding that a man had to work. He was always an old man in his mind.

In the workplace, it is easy to feel overwhelmed. It is easy to look at some-one else's responsibilities and feel like you are doing more work, and they are just at work to socialize. If you ever find yourself feeling these things, you are just experiencing symptoms of "minding others' business." The sooner you can check yourself and realize that you are getting paid to do a job, and they are getting paid to do their job, and the one does not affect the other, then you will be able to get back to the core purpose of you being in that environment. You are not there by happenstance; you are there on assignment. This assignment can be for the purpose of building character in you or to impact others. Sometimes you will not know. I encourage you to stay close to Yeshua, stay focused on the task(s) at hand, and do not get distracted or weary or fearful of what is around you.

In Matthew 14:28–31, And Peter answered him, "Lord, if it is you, command me to come to you on the water." He said, "Come." So, Peter got out of the boat and walked on the water and came to Jesus. But when he saw the wind,[a] he was afraid, and beginning to sink he cried out, "Lord, save me." Jesus immediately reached out his hand and took hold of him, saying to him, "O you of little faith, why did you doubt?" Have faith in your relationship with God enough to understand that He is with you.

This task was difficult for me to learn. In one of my positions, I can say that I did not have my focus on God the entire time. Things were fresh, it was a new position, and I was excited about the opportunity. While in the role, things began to shake in the organization—new CEO, new location, five new managers within a year. I could not grasp what was happening around me. Every day I came to work, I would say, "For your glory, God." I was spiritually drained and insecure. The job was unstable, and everyone was looking for someone to blame for gaps in operations. It took me getting sick, losing time, losing sleep, and failed attempts of getting affirmation from mankind for me to realize that I had completely forgotten who the captain of my ship is. I had to take inventory of my heart, my mindset, and my daily prayers to realize that I was living reactively and not faithfully. I had my hands on the wheel of the ship when I was riding through the storm. Just like Peter, I lost faith, somewhere along the ride, and I was drowning. When I made this discovery about myself, I moved from feeling undervalued to being numb. I moved from being numb to being angry at God for leaving me in my situation. "Do you not see what they are doing to me?" I would say to God. "I have a son to care for. I have goals and dreams that I need to pursue, but I am an emotional wreck!"

I prayed, I cried, I ate honey buns; I was still on the ship in the fog. I finally stopped. I had to be still and listen. Stop begging God to remove me from the company. Slow down on the job applications. Stop going from cubicle to cubicle to try and "talk out my problems," hoping God would talk through my peers. Twelve gained pounds later, with acne-polluted skin and feeling hypersensitive, I apologized. I repented for my lack of faith. Who was I to be angry when, all this time, the reason my ship was still in the fog was because I was trying to steer without directions or insight and instruction?

If you find yourself in this place, I want you to realize, first and foremost, God has not abandoned you. He wants you to trust in Him, and trust that where He has placed you is a suitable fit for what He has put inside of you. What does that mean? You have everything inside of you to complete the task at hand. What is the task? I cannot answer that. What I can recommend is that you do not take the workplace lightly or perceive it as a place just to make money. God does not need your career to feed you. Look out the window. There was just a bird that shouted, "Hallelujah, amen." God wants to get so close to you and have you confide in Him, and be intimate with Him. Have faith that God loves you and wants you to be free in Him. And that means you are being the best version of you that you can be. That version of you will bring glory to Him, help those around you, and ultimately feel good in the innermost parts of your being.

I love you, Brent, and miss you dearly.

Where Are the Birds Going?

Have you ever heard someone talking about smelling the rain? It is a real thing. If a storm is coming, a downpour, you can sometimes smell the rain before it falls. What does that smell like, or when does one get used to the "smell" of rain? There is no precise scientific description. It's just a scent that you get used to after the evidence of the storm; you then know what to look for. This theory is good in hindsight, but because you do not know in advance what you are looking for, or rather smelling for, you will not know what the smell of rain really is. What can you do to prepare for the storm if you are unaware of it coming toward you? What other things are present to tell you there is something on the horizon?

I would always joke about animals in the movie *Twister*. Or, if you are not aware of that reference, how about the historical Noah's ark? Somehow, the animals always know that something is coming. One telltale sign of a storm coming is the evidence of birds in the sky. They will always let you know something is brewing from above. I'm sure there is an instinctual reason for their response, but metaphorically, they are also in the sky. High above the areas that will soon be affected by the wind, the rain, the lightning.

When I was a child, any time I would see clouds coming in, I would get still and look up. I was looking for the birds' response time and direction of flight. If the clouds were coming in from the south, and the birds would fly in a circular motion, I knew we may get rain, but it was not serious enough for me to take cover. If the clouds were coming in from the south and the birds flew north, however, I knew a storm was coming. Most of the time, it was not just a quick storm, but one worthy of the birds leaving their nests and familiar nests to relocate. In any organization, likewise, there is a budget for turnover or attrition. The organization understands that life happens, and people change directions. The organization will also plan for errors and performance management up to and equal to termination (have we not all heard that before?). Why are we talking about planned attrition? I want people to understand that associates leaving an organization is equivalent to birds flying in a circular motion when there is a quick shower brewing. This will alert you to a possible change that may or may not have a direct impact on your day-to-day responsibilities.

When there are managers leaving an organization, or people in positions who are aware of changes coming—for example, human resources, project management, and engineers—those are the times to pay attention to the birds. Who are the birds? They are the employees who make, or are involved with making, decisions that are pivotal to the organization's successes or failures, profits or losses.

Transferrable Lessons

1. What should you do?

   Understand, it is important to ask questions about the direction of the organization. You should feel free to have that conversation with your manager. If you are not comfortable with your direct manager, change that. I'm not talking about being best friends, but you should always be comfortable talking to your manager about your current position, the assessment of your performance, and the future of your bread and butter—your career.

2. What should you not do?

   Put your pipe dreams in front of reality. The reality is that we all start in an organization with a few goals in mind:

   a. To create opportunities in a career doing something we love and in which we see growth potential.

   b. To use the opportunity as a stepping-stone to develop our skill set, build our resume, or network with professionals.

   c. To make more money.

Many times, as professionals, we have a couple of options of how to build a career portfolio. We can take jobs at a range of organizations to gain experience, exposure, and insight into doing what we desire. We can stay at one organization and climb the invisible "ladder." Or we can have a main job with multiple small jobs on the side that will help us be versatile and network. I encourage everyone to find and do the thing that fits their ideal of what a career should be for them.

When strategizing or mastering your approach to your professional career or purpose, remember that you come first. For me, that was a tough lesson to learn. Coming from a country town, we are taught that the community is everything. "Two is stronger than one." "It takes a community to raise a child." "If two or more gather in my name, there am I with them." Okay, that last one always stands. When working at a J-O-B, you must remember that most of the time, you are there for a purpose seen and unseen. One is for you to be readily available to Yeshua to use you as a vessel to impact others or grow your character, and the other reason if for you to make money to be able to enjoy the leisure of life, give back to the community, and to buy toys and land.

When you work for large corporations, you will discover that they spend money on what they value. I discovered there are positions that I did not even know exist! There are human resource positions and strategies for employee relations, internal investigations, and more. These all sounded familiar until I discovered that there is money being spent to train managers on how to sell the associates on the dream of what is next. They are paid to minimize real concerns and maximize the potential of what is to come with your future in the organization. If you listen closely, the competencies or behavioral language will be used to train the associates to conform to what the corporation's direction is now and/or to redirect the associates' focus, hiding concerns that could directly impact your career.

Not to demonize all the goals of an organization, but everything that I mentioned may now have you thinking, "How can I be better for the goals of the organization?" as opposed to, "How can I be better for my goals for my career? How do the values of this corporation align with my dream/purpose?" When you forget the reason why you are working, you are working to survive.

You begin to feed into the potentially toxic or misaligned culture of where you are and forget where you are heading. Also, in that frame of mind, you begin to live for temporal benefits like paid time off, parking spots, bonuses, and cookouts rather than remembering the overarching goal. When we spend a lot of time with an organization, we begin to feel as if we are the organization. But we are not. We are an employee seeking a dream, aiming for a goal.

How does this tie in with the birds? I mentioned earlier that the birds are the employees who make, or are involved with making, decisions that are pivotal to the organization's successes or failures, profits or losses. Pay attention to the direction of the birds. Learn when to take cover, when to weather the storm, or when it is time to relocate and realign to your personal and professional goals, even if that means leaving a place where you built a nest.

Mosquitoes and Garden Hoe

One of the advantages of growing up country is that you get an early lesson of working hard and enjoying the benefits of your labor. At a tender age, I can recall seeing my grandfather plowing the ground with his fancy tractors, and my grandmother working alongside him putting something in the dirt. With her hair tied, large boots, and super large gloves, Little Lady would work the field sun-up to sun-down with the hope and belief that, one day, you will see something come up, something green, something unexpected by the passersby.

Let me tell you a story. When I was in kindergarten, I would go to school half a day. When the day was over, I would ride the bus for what seemed like an hour to all the passenger stops. Usually, when Mrs. George, my bus driver, arrived at my stop, I was sound asleep. She would always stop to speak to Little Lady, who would walk to the road with her gloves on and her hair tied. I would wake to the sound of her raspy little voice and cute giggle.

After the bus driver would leave, my Little Lady would ask me how my day was, and as I carried on about building cars to race and crayons, we would walk inside to make my daily sandwich. The sandwich was filled with fresh deli meat, cheese, mayo and lettuce, and then we would pop it in the toaster. I would have juice or water, and then it was time to go back outside. This was usually my favorite part of the day—my Little Lady showing me the ropes that would last me a lifetime. We were not only planting seeds. It was more involved than that. We had to prep the ground, work the ground, plant the seed, and water the ground. Days after the seed was planted, I never even went to inspect for sprouts. We would go back outside to work a new field and repeat the same tasks. When we were done planting new seed in the new field, we would return to the previous field to inspect the ground for intruders: weeds. If the wind blew, and carried grass seed to your soiled ground, you could expect to see weeds. But no worries. I would pull them up or hoe them down and remove them from our ground.

As we were working the ground, I could smell the supper cooking, and I could hear the neighborhood coming back to life with people coming home. This made me sad. I loved spending one-on-one time with my grandmother. She taught me how to work, she taught me how to think, and she taught me how to tell stories. She would talk cheerfully about what it was like growing up in South Carolina, and all her struggles and victories. My Little Lady, she will tell it like it is. There were some idiots, fools, and silly people in those stories, and I loved it. After we were done in the field, it was time to take her clothes off the line.

We would remove our gloves and she would go in the house to retrieve her baskets. I would sit on the gas tank like a horse and absorb all the warmth from it basking in the sun. As she removed the wood pins that were holding up her clothes, she would continue to tell me stories of her life, and she would tell me about silly things my grandfather and uncle did the day before. It was the funniest thing to listen to my grandmother talk because she is a small yet sassy lady, but also soothing. So much so that sometimes, as I listened to her speak, I would lie in the grass and look up at the pecan tree and the pear tree. The breeze would dance with the leaves. I could hear the duck quacking and the cats meowing in the close distance. Little Lady's clothes smelled of soft bleach, and my mind would visualize what she was explaining. This was the perfect recipe for a nap under the sun. Most of the time, I would be awakened by either the phrase of "No, ma'am; it's time to work," or "This girl done fell asleep." Either way, it was the best nap ever.

As I began to age, my grandmother's work ethic did not. She would still work the garden, cut up firewood, and hang clothes on the line, just at a slower pace. Yes, my grandfather was around, but she did not like when he interrupted her routine. She knew that to get things, you had to work. My Little Lady's yard was and still is the best-looking yard in the neighborhood. Her fruit trees still reap fruit—pears, peaches, and we just found pomegranates! Figs, grapes, and pecans. Her gardens and fields would harvest sugarcane, peanuts, field peas, greens, and my favorite, okra. No, honestly—why is okra a thing?

As a child, I remember the garden yielding a large harvest. Although I watched my grandmother and grandfather constantly work the fields and plow the ground, it was still always amazing to see the fruits and vegetables their efforts would reap. One day you would see dirt, one day you would see a flower, and over the next couple of months you would see enough of a harvest to feed the neighborhood. My grandmother would call my parents and say, "You better come get some of these vegetables; it's too much for us to contain in our freezer." We would go to my grandparents' house with paint mixer buckets and fill those with peanuts. We would have baskets for the field peas, and they would cut the okra to torture me with—okay, it is not about me. We would all sit around and have conversation, snap the peas, wash the harvest, and store them in freezer bags to enjoy throughout the fall and winter.

When planting seed, it is important to take into consideration the season. Each seed has specifications of the weather requirements to allow germination. The knowledge of the temperature to support that seed is critical. The temperature affects the plant's growth. Some reasons why planting can be unsuccessful include: overwatering, the temperature being wrong, the seed being bad, and planting in the wrong soil or not tilling the land.

Timing and research were necessary to my grandparents' farming success. To my eyes, I saw them tilling, riding the tractor, pulling weeds, and putting up fake owls and crows to scare invaders (animals). But I never considered or was mature enough to understand the years of trial and error, money spent and lost, relationships to gain information, and physical labor needed to get a good harvest. When I helped in the land, there was an over-harvest, too much for them to store and eat.

As a child, I never saw my parents sit around and not work. I never can recall my grandmother complain that she was tired. I never remember not having a chore, yet I never remember being hungry. I was never homeless. I never went without. Everyone had a job to do, and if I wanted to hurry up so I could read my books, I had to do mine. Everyone was good at something.

In my home growing up, we all had chores. My mother strategically assigned weekly chores for her three daughters to manage around the house. Not only did it allow her time to work and spend time with her husband, but it also gave us responsibility. My brother, who was the oldest, bless his heart, always had to cut the grass and throw out the trash. My brother was not even allowed in the home until the sun was setting. Outside of our chores, we also had things that we enjoyed doing. My brother always seemed to get in trouble for taking electronics apart and putting them back together. Now, we were in the country, and as you can imagine, we did not have the most money. So, when my father saw the family stereo dissected, you could imagine the discontent. But, by them allowing him to do this, staying outdoors, and working with my father in construction, my brother made money in high school building car systems with amps and speaker boxes. He is now the owner/founder of All Deeds, a construction/electronics company. My oldest sister, other than arguing with me (Hey, Sis!), was always cooking up something. She would spend her days learning how to bake and cook by hanging with our grandmothers. She loved mature conversations and stayed out of trouble. She was very observant and was able to retain facts easily. She is now a mother and wife. She bakes for special occasions and is working to begin baking for her own business. My mid-sister, slightly older than me, well, she was a risk taker and a penny pincher. No, literally. She would find coins all over the place and squirrel them away in her raggedy purse. She would not leave home without her bag. It never ceased to amaze me the way my sister would pull out that purse and drop her coins into her purple container that had to have a million coins in it. If you ever asked her, she was always "broke," but if she saw something she wanted, she would reach inside her purple container and count it up.

Perhaps unsurprisingly, she grew up to be a finance director/program manager. That leaves me, the wanderer/artist. As a child, I would always get lost in the wind. I would finish my chores, just so I could go wander and create or do something new. My father worked at a wood shop down the road. I would go in that shop and find pieces of wood to create stuff with and to decorate the home. I would move furniture around every day pursuing my vision of interior design. The other things I would do is entertain by acting, read books, and take my naps. I am now writing this book, styling homes for a side gig, and still napping like a pro.

All of this sounds chummy and glorious, but how does it relate to the workforce? Easy! You will reap what you sow. You will grow where you plant seeds/time. Your hard work will produce something, but are you working hard in the right area?

In corporations, there are many influences. Departments, sub-departments, teams, and silos. When you apply for a position, you read the job description and may think, "Wow, that is something I want to do." You go into the interview, they like you, offer you the job, and two weeks and a drug test later, you find yourself in your new cubicle. It is an exciting thing, like the first day of school. In the position, you must identify and lay down the law regarding some especially important things.

Transferable Lessons

1. Prep the ground

   To prepare for any project or long-term goal, it takes research and an understanding of resources. If you are anything like me, you are a visionary. I have been blessed with the ability to come up with workable solutions for solving problems. I can see where we are now and where we can be if we modify procedures. It is a pain for me to sit still long enough to plan the minute details of an operation, though. Surprisingly enough, I got paid to do this for many years, but the before and after is what really excites me. Understanding what you are good at and what you are not good at is a major part of preparing the ground. Being not so good at something does not mean you are less than capable. It means you must be able to form relationships, know what resources are available, and understand where and how to obtain them.

   There are three basic questions that you should be able to answer while preparing the ground:

   a. What are we doing and what is the end goal(s)? It is important to identify if you are implementing something new or if you are improving on an already existing process. If you are implementing something new in your organization, you are tilling new land that has not been cleared. Though this process is adventurous, it can also bring challenges of gaining the buy-in of investors and potential customers and building trusted relationships with strategic vendors. Personally, I love tilling new land. It allows me space to be creative and strategic with creating business models.

When improving on an existing process, you should be prepared to understand the land, the current seeds and weeds or standard of work that has benefited or harmed the organization. Be strategic in how you approach what needs to be done to make a process more efficient and be sure you understand waste and what adds value to the goal, consumers, and the business. This will be your main priority when preparing for implementation.

b. A lesson learned in grade school, the five Ws, is a concept that should be used whenever starting or changing a system or project: Who, What, When Where and Why. So simple but imperative to understand what can be completed by you and what needs to be outsourced. I will keep reiterating this point ----start out this way when beginning a business if you plan to appropriately scale your business to accommodate growth.

A tool that I used when working on an assignment is the practice of doing, delegating, deleting, or delaying. As mentioned, know your strengths and your limits without shame. Identify what you can do; what you need to delegate or outsource; what is important, but not at this point of the schedule; and what adds no value and needs to be deleted.

c. Can I do this? Is this goal even obtainable? Let us be honest. If I could insert the number of ideas that I attempted to implement, but did not appropriately prepare the land for, you would laugh. I gave myself an out every time. You know, I am not the strategic sibling, so my creative juices won't allow me to plan appropriately. Or maybe I can sell my ideas and walk away from the work of making this happen and seeing it through. Have you ever entertained thoughts like these?

Well, let me tell you. If those are your thoughts when beginning a project, just walk away! Life is oh so precious and sweet, and it has an expiration date for all of us. Don't consume your energy planting seed in a ground that has not been prepared. Enjoy the harvest of others in that specialty. That is okay as well! But if you are attempting to do something because you are passionate about it, you must see it through. Follow steps 1 and 2 above. Identify your goal, what good looks like. Identify your five Ws, which should list your resources, your people, your timeline and schedules, and your why. Once you are here in the sowing process, take one step at a time. Try not to skip steps and acknowledge that this is hard. When you see those commercials of farmers, you see them wiping the sweat from their brow. Not only do they have to produce in nice weather, but they must push through both the hot days and the cold, wet days. Not only do they have to drive those cool-looking tractors, but they must maintain them and keep them gassed. Not only do they have to plant the seed, but they must purchase the seed, the fertilizer, the tools to work the land and pray that the result is a sprout. Indeed, to see that small green sprout is satisfying, but it is only the beginning. They must protect the sprout from animals above and below the surface, from fungus and weeds! The process does not stop, and it is not easy. But once you say you can do it, fight the good fight. Understand that a bad day is just that day. And a doubtful thought is just that thought. Prepare the land, prepare your mind, and prepare for the harvest!

Mudbone House Rules

There was not a full year in my childhood that my family did not own a dog. Golden Retriever, Labrador, Weimaraner, English Spaniel, English Boxer pit mix, and your occasional mut that we found or that found us. My father, being a contractor, would build a doghouse with scrap materials and set the dog up nice in the back. Every day, my father would greet the dog first thing in the morning as he loaded his work truck, and again in the evening when he returned from work. Each dog had its own personality and favorite member of the family, although my father was usually the one who fed them.

Mudbone was my father's dog. He was a Weimaraner that came to my father on a construction site, and never left. I remember when my father brought him home. He had the biggest ears and the most discerning eyes. I felt like he knew what you were feeling. He was not a high maintenance dog, but because I was so young, I loved giving him attention. This is horrible, but I would ride his back like a horse. I was a young'un, and I had a belly that I loved laying on his warm back. When he would be annoyed with me, he would get up and attempt to walk away. Little did he know, I was not done loving on him. I would hold on to his neck. When I became too heavy to do such a thing, he began lying on his back for whatever reason.

Though he was my father's love, everyone in the family has their own favorite memories of experiences with Mudbone. I am no exception. When I was growing up, there were neighbors to the left, right, front, and back of us. Many of them had animals for food or as pets. Their yards had gardens and field rows with produce. One neighbor resided near Mudbone's doghouse. He owned pigs and hogs—oh, the smells. Well, I do not believe Mudbone enjoyed the smell or the sounds. One day, we were heading to the beach. It was a rare occasion to have my father pull away from his work, so we were all super prepared and excited. We didn't want to chance not being ready to go when my father was ready. One thing my father always did when we took long trips and beach trips was to load the cooler. Man! The sandwich variety, the snacks, Snapple, and always for my father mixed nuts or candied Boston baked beans. Depending on the beach location, we would take food to grill, hot dog buns, and hamburger condiments. It was always a blast to see my mother wear a T-shirt dress instead of scrubs and to see my father pull out his gold chain and Hawaiian shirts; they were adorable.

As my father was loading the van to head to the beach, I could hear him fussing at Mudbone. I ran to see what was going on because this did not usually happen. As I approached the scene, I could see we had a situation. Mudbone had one eye squinting at my father, and he kept trying to turn away. He was also holding his mouth in a weird manner. Attempting to help, I popped Mud on his back and said bad dog. My father continued to pull Mudbone's head toward him and slowly pried his mouth open. Finally! That was when a wet, still piglet hit the ground. I never thought I could be so upset with a dog. "Mudbone!!! What are you doing?" My father was so disappointed. I could see it in his eyes, and I thought we were not going to be able to go to the beach. But he walked across the field to inform our neighbor that one of his pigs got into our dog's yard, and it did not end well. Mudbone knew he was in trouble, and he went to his house to stay out of the way. Soon enough, my father and his dog were back on good terms, and he never ate another pig.

Not only do dogs eat pigs, but they know how to weed out snakes. They almost enjoy exposing what can be of harm to you. I had a dog named Pinky. Pinky was a boxer pit mix, and such a happy boy. He also had a luxurious suite outdoors, in a prime location that offered him a front-row seat to witness animals and humans enter and leave the premises. Every morning, in his young years, I would look out the kitchen window, just to be greeted by the beautiful stare of him. He was white with brown spots, very attentive, and always ready to go. He would jump in my Toyota Corolla to ride around town, for no reason at all, and he was all good with playing catch with me. I would have loved to play fetch, but the dog did not know how to give me the ball back. Instead, he loved to be chased. He would get the softball and begin to run around the trees and his doghouse. People said it was his face, but I swear he was laughing at my attempts to get the ball back. Pinky was my boy; he was a gift that my father gave me when my mid-sister left the house for college. He thought it would be a good idea for me to have a friend. Pinky stayed with me inside for a couple of months before my mother caught on that he did not need to be bottle-fed any longer. It was a sad day when he got evicted. One thing about my childhood—dogs did not stay in the house. They had their own house out in the yard.

I still had long days with him in the sun, and when it was cold, he would just so happen to be in the house with me, snuggled by the fireplace. Pinky was a gentle dog, but he loved excitement. He loved fireworks and he loved to let you know when he caught something in his house. Puppies and cats, squirrels, you name it, they were all drawn to him, and I believe some days, he protected them in a paternal way. He would snuggle with the kittens to keep them warm. He would scoot the stray puppies away with his large paw when they tried to eat his food. He was a nice guy until he saw something he did not trust.

One day when I was getting water and peering out the window to catch his morning stare—it was not there. Instead, I witnessed Pinky patting the ground in a rhythm. It was a pat, pat, swoop, pat, pat, bite. He repeated that for a while until I saw something being thrown from one end of the yard to the next. I then witnessed Pinky shaking this thing from left to right. After about two minutes, he stopped. He sat down in his yard to rest. I thought it would be a good idea to go inspect the scene and see what was happening. As soon as I touched the screen door, Pinky jumped up and began to prance like a prince horse in pride of his kill. I was worried and anxious because I never thought he would kill a cat or another animal. The closer I got to him, I noticed that his tongue was dry and his face was huge! Oh my gracious, he'd played with and killed a venomous snake. Appearing to see my surprise, he went and retrieved his kill and brought it to me. What a big snake! He again began to prance. I ran to get my father so he could inspect the snake to ensure it was dead, then I ran back to check on Pinky, giving him the good-boy pat and affirmations that he wanted. He was genuinely happy. Not only had he killed the snake, but he protected his family, and he had a blast doing it. Pinky's face stayed swollen for a week after the kill, and he smiled throughout the healing process.

Transferrable Lessons

1. Loyal partners

   Today, I have—well, my son has—a dog. This dog lives in the house with us. He is a mischievous old man who clearly knows right from wrong, but he continues to test boundaries. When he joined my family, he was four years old with a personality and experiences in tow. The bond between us was a rocky one because he did not trust me and I did not trust him on my beautiful rug collection.

   Throughout the years, we spent increased time together and established new commands. He understood house rules and he learned his position. Did he continue to pee on my rugs from time to time? Absolutely. Did I throw him away or take him to the pound? Absolutely not.

   Dogs can teach you many things about patience and responsibility, and they can show you how clean you really are when you "think" you closed the trash can. The most rewarding and unforgettable thing about dogs in my life is their loyalty. Dogs are loyal to you when you are not the nicest, not the most energized, and do not have time to take them for the long walks that were promised. In this section, I explained to you how my father met Mudbone, and how important he was to him. He was important to my father because the dog was always there. Even when he died, he would not let go until my father was there.

In organizations, there will be peers and managers who are loyal to you, the company, or both. The people who are loyal to the organization will not let pigs, snakes, or anything harmful go unnoticed. Their job is to expose it—or you, if necessary—and ensure that the organization can move forward. This person is your best friend. How can someone who exposes me be my best friend? It is called accountability and reality. It is easy to go about life unchecked, or only receiving praise. That is unrealistic and I am sorry to tell you it's a lie. There is no human being on this earth who is perfect. If you meet this person, and they do not agree with you and you know you are right, you have a decision to make. You need to first evaluate if what is important to you is important to the organization. In no company will you agree with everything they do one hundred percent of the time. But if you are a save-the-animals advocate working for a meat factory, we may have a conflict here.

Identify what the core values are of the organization and identify the person who can help keep you accountable to perform at your best while you are in that infrastructure. The organization's core values will not likely change because you do not agree with them or because they hurt your feelings.

2. He stayed with me inside for a couple of months

In my experience, it is best to identify who the key players, decision makers, and long-termers in an organization are. Once you identify who these individuals are, develop a professional relationship with them. A professional relationship is different from a personal one because, in a professional relationship, the driving force is to accomplish a common goal, to represent a common cause, and to present a common agenda. When developing relationships, allow your personality to show and your opinions to stay at a minimum.

When I had my dog with me indoors, he ate, drank his milk, and stayed in his blanket to keep warm. He soaked in all the information I was providing him about how to survive and he watched my mannerisms, how I communicated, and what I was saying. Staying close to me allowed him to develop an understanding that I was a resource for his food, and I was his master. Identifying your "master" and resources in an organization is imperative for operational excellence and functionality. Remember earlier we discussed not trying to do it all. Why go into an organization and try to waste a lot of time for no reason when someone else more than likely already gets paid to do, or enjoys doing, something that can help you succeed on your project? Spend time being a sponge and learning the latest information. I promise, you will have many opportunities in an established organization to present your ideas and to let your skills shine!

3. Giving him the good-boy pat and affirmations that he wanted:

As with Mudbone, knowing how to receive and give a "good-boy pat" is a weapon not to be taken lightly. Understanding and acting on love languages plays a major key in organizational success. When working among business professionals, everyone can make it seem that it is easy to do their job—so easy that it appears effortless. Some people believe when something is done effortlessly, there is no need to celebrate successes. But the smallest tasks sometimes can be the most difficult to accomplish. Whether it was difficult to remain consistent over a long period of time, or the person completing the task knows how to mask the hardship, it took work. While you are getting acclimated to your new team, make sure to learn how they like to receive praise and then weave that into the interactions. Some may appreciate a small coffee; some may like a hug or a fist bump. Some prefer organizational announcements to be presented verbally, while others prefer them to be in written form. Some would like for you to make eye contact and continue to do your job. Whatever the case, let the people around you know you see and appreciate them. Do not let good works go unnoticed.

Fishing for Bait

Waking up to a sunny day in the country was confirmation from God that today was going to be full of adventures. The best part about growing up country is the access to the land—seeing your harvest and living off it.

One seed that my grandfather had sown was digging ponds on his acreage. Going to my grandparents' house, you would hear the fountain going, and you would see him fertilizing the water. From my perspective as a child, the fountain was there for aesthetics; it looked pretty. As an adult, I now understand it was to ensure that the water was fertilized and kept clear of pond grass and pine needles. When I was a young girl, two or three years old, I learned how to fish. My grandfather was a teacher of skills. He taught many people the skills of building, wood crafting, gardening . . . and fishing. When he was in teaching mode, he would take it step by step, and he would not talk much in between about irrelevant information. I observed my grandmother and grandfather fishing. Their fishing rods were made of sugarcane and string. No reel, no fancy buttons. When fishing with them, I saw the bobbin dancing in the water, experienced the long wait while sitting on buckets, and sometimes heard stories of their childhood.

"Oh!" I would think. "I have this in the bag. All I have to do is sit here, hold this rod or prop it up until that float disappears, and then we'll have a fish fry for dinner." As my grandfather would fish, I would lean in on his shoulder. One day, he looked at me and asked, "Do you want to have at it?"

"Of course," I said yes with so much confidence. I started to move the rod that he already had in the water.

"Wait a minute now," he said. "You is moving too much. You have to get balanced."

He allowed me to hold his rod as he went to string a new one. He sat next to me and told me that fishing is a sport, which a lot of people were going to experience but not master. As he talked, I remember thinking, "What is there to master? It is extremely easy to do this. You hold a stick at a ninety-degree angle to the water, and you do not let go." As we sat there, I watched his bobbin begin to dance in the water, then stop. He just said, "Mm hmm, the babies are playing in this area; let's go over here."

I asked, "Why can't we stay here?"

He explained, "The baby fish and the larger fish will not stay in the same area. Momma is looking for food right now—she is on the hunt."

We both got up and moved our buckets to the other side of the pond, in the sun! Man, it was suddenly a curse to have the sun out. I did not complain aloud, of course. When we set up shop, my grandfather's line began to dance again. I could not believe it. I was excited and yet concerned. Why were the fish drawn to his line and not mine? That bobbin danced and danced and danced. This time I could tell it was not a tadpole or baby fish. Bertha was on the line. The float did one more dip but this time never came back up. My grandfather jumped up and began yell, "Uh-huh!! Come on!" He finally pulled the rod up, and out of the water came a freshwater bluegill, gasping for air. I could see its fins opening and closing, and from my young perspective I focused on its eyes, which were full of fear. Grandaddy grabbed the fish with his big oily hands and asked, "Do you know how to unhook the catch?"

I said no, and he began to teach. He told me to always take my time when removing the fish from the hook. You don't want to hurt the fish. In my mind, that was the craziest thing he said to me. What if I did hurt the fish? We were about to eat it anyways! Once you remove the hook from the gills, you throw it in a covered bucket of water in the shade. You did not want to start a broil with the bucket in the sun. He proceeded to get more bait for his hook and cast his rod in the water again.

We did this dance for about an hour. Grandaddy kept catching fish and catching fish. My excitement grew and went away each time he re-casted his rod. I would occasionally pull my rod out of the water to make sure the bait had not disintegrated—we'd been there for so long. Granddaddy caught enough fish to feed the family, and I caught nothing. Feeling defeated, I cleaned up my rod, picked up our cups that had once held ice, and carried the tools, while he carried the bucket of dancing fish. He looked at me and said, "Don't be mad. You have to learn how to fish before you start catching fish."

I remember saying, "All I had to do was stand there. That's all you did!"

He laughed and responded, "No, that is all you saw me doing. There is more to fishing that just standing by the pond and waiting for the fish to find your bait. You first have to find your bait, string your rod, find the water to cast your rod, wait for the right timing, and discover where the fish is in the water by paying attention to the reaction of the other creatures in and around the water. You have to understand the weather, and most importantly, you have to hold your mouth right."

Now, I understood maybe sixty-five percent of what he was saying, including all the prep work, which in my little mind I was going to show him I knew how to work. But hold my mouth right? This man had lost his mind. "Granddaddy, will it be okay with you for me to practice if you are not here?"

"Yes, you can do all the prep work, but I do not want you by the pond by yourself. If you want to fish and I am not here, ask your grandmother to sit with you. But one thing you need to start doing—well, actually two things: Learn how to find your bait and string your rod. You can always do that while you wait for me."

As significant as that was, at the time, I saw this as an opportunity to show my grandfather that I could do this. He showed me some spots in the yard that were bait beds, as he called them, and then gave me the green light to dig away. That day, we enjoyed his fish, and I knew deep within that I would be enjoying my fish soon. I just had to find my bait.

After I convinced my mid-sister that her adventures were no longer fun for the day, I got her to invest in my ideas. We found some Tupperware—sorry, Mom—and ran out the back door, ready for an adventure. We crossed over to my grandparents' property and I showed her the lay of the land, directing her to one of the bait beds. "Are we supposed to use our hands?"

"I'm not sure," I answered. "Let's go find Little Lady's hoe or hand digger." After we had all our tools, we started to dig. The hoe idea was not the best. We found some bait, but the hoe cut those suckers in half. The great news is, they were still moving. The sad news is, we had to use our hands. Everything seemed cleaner back then, even the dirt and the environment around the dirt.

Anyway, after we had enough worms to feed the nation in the pond, we went to go look for the rods. That was when I remembered—oh no! We couldn't go to the water without Granddaddy. So, we put our Tupperware container by the bait bed and said if they escaped, at least they wouldn't get far. At least we knew how to find our bait. That was a lot of work. We had to be digging for an hour. I was starting to understand Grandaddy's statement that all I SAW was him standing here, but there was work involved.

Along and along, our schedules began to match, and my grandfather was more than excited to help me learn how to fish. It offered us time to chat, provided him with many laughs, and gave me a lot of heartaches. You see, when I began catching fish, they were babies, and one thing about my grandfather and fishing—if the fish were the wrong size, or the wrong fish, he would make you throw it back in the water. That was heartbreaking! A fish is a fish is a fish! But, no, you had gone there to catch a particular fish, and you could only leave with that fish.

One day, I was relaxed, enjoying the shade, drinking my Little Lady's sugar with lemonade and ice (that's too-sweet lemonade), and I was getting quite a few nibbles on my hook. I was beginning to get a little too anxious about catching the right fish that day, but I just had a feeling it was about to happen. Two hours and no bites later, I spent the day witnessing everyone else at the pond catch fish. Everyone but me, but I did not care; I was not leaving. Everyone began to leave. As I sat there determined, I saw my granddad come my way. I thought he was going to tell me I could not be at the pond alone, but instead, he pulled up his bucket next to me. He sat there, looked at me, and said, "You know why you're not catching fish?"

I looked at him defeated, and said, "No."

He laughed. "Look at you. You're not holding your mouth right."

"What does that even mean, Grandaddy?"

"That fish don't want to come out and see that ugly face. Look at me— this is how you look while you wait." He went on to screw up his face in a pouty way.

"Yeah, okay, Granddaddy," I said, laughing.

"Fix your mouth, and you will catch your fish. You must learn how to wait, without losing hope that you will catch your fish. Hold your mouth right."

"That crazy man," I thought. But as crazy as he was when I began to go fishing, I did start to wait patiently, and I began to enjoy my time waiting. Eventually, I caught my fair share of fish, but the first time I almost fell in. Okay, I will tell you about that.

I was out there with my mid-sister. My float went under. And I mean, it went under. I knew it was a huge fish. I squealed, as I was being pulled into the pond grass surrounding the pond. My sister ran to me and jumped behind me and began to pull. We counted and pulled, counted and pulled, until, finally, we saw the fish flapping on the bank with us. We caught a bass!! And a huge one at that. I was so excited that day. Grandaddy took pictures as we cheesed. Bass was the sweetest meat in the pond, and I could smell the fish frying in my imagination. Yes, I smelled it sizzling right up until my grandfather said, "Now throw it back."

I yelled, "What! Why?"

He looked at me, smiled, and gently said, "Because that is not what you went to catch. No matter how sweet it may be, stay focused on what you are doing. Don't get so caught up in the size of the prize you were not trying to win."

I was so mad that day. That was the first time I was ever mad at this man. I learned the skill of finding my bait, I learned how to string the rod, I learned how to hold my mouth, and the day I get my catch, he made me throw it back. The nerve!

That same day, I caught other fish, and he taught me how to clean the fish and prepare them for the cook (Little Lady). "We all do our part," he said, "and you did well." Even though I was still in my feelings about the bass, the bluegill, fries, and other food was so enjoyable.

Transferrable Lessons

There are a lot of key points in this section that shaped how I approached seeking new levels and stages in my life. I would like to take the time to point them out in case you overlooked them, and yes, we are going to get scriptural.

1. Fish drawn to his line:

   The story of the miraculous catch in John 21 in the Bible tells us how Yeshua instructed His disciples to cast their nets on the right side of the boat while fishing in the Sea of Galilee. The disciples had been fishing all night without any success of catching fish. When they listened to Jesus's instruction and cast their net on a different side of the boat, they made a great catch. The catch was so large it was hard for them to haul it in. As hard as it was to pull in the catch, Jesus then asked for some of the fish. When they brought the fish in, they did not tear the net.

   Wow. Let us dissect this and discover how this is applicable to everyday life and working within an organization. The disciples, in their own will, knew that they needed to eat. To eat, the disciples went fishing. In the natural, we understand that to have resources to feed our flesh, we need to move and act because faith without works is dead. If I have faith that I will eat, but I do not take action to buy, catch, or ask for food, I will remain hungry. The scripture does not speak on this in this context, but if you follow and study the life of Christ, you will find that during this time, Christ and his disciples were fishers of men. The skill of fishing was something that they had to discuss, master, and use to introduce the truth and the light to many men in flesh and in spirit. In my studies, there is no evidence that the disciples were lacking in the skills necessary to catch the fish. But on that day, they were unsuccessful. They went out the next day and they met a man that they did not recognize on the shore. He asked, "Friends, haven't you any fish?" "No," they answered. He said, "Throw your nets on the right side of the boat and you will find some." (John 21)

2. Being obedient is your purpose and will make a way for you

The disciples HEARD the instruction, and they were adaptable and open. I imagine them thinking, "Why not give it a try? What we tried at first did not work. The fish are not drawn to our net. We're hungry for a catch." When the disciples listened and threw their net as instructed, the fish began to fill the net so much, they were unable to haul in the catch because of its abundance.

Wow! Not only were the men at work and about their business, but because they were not bitter or hardened due to their circumstance, they were able to hear God. There are so many situations I've endured, that I can say that my heart should have been hardened. In the flesh, I saw how I was looked over. I saw the sacrifices that I made to position myself to be a blessing to my family financially. I could experience the memories of hardship repeatedly when I moved to a new city in hopes that a company would fulfill their commitment and then fail me. I did not allow this to harden my heart.

I remember one experience, when my son was really getting involved with sports. I had to buy him new equipment and a new bag. I held it off for so long, but I did not want him to know that money was tight. I did what I needed to do, paid all my bills, and looked in my account. I had $2.15 in my possession. I did not know what I would do, but I knew that God had me. I did not break down thinking about letdowns at work. I did not lose sight of the empty nets without fish. I simply remained hungry for a catch and continued to go fishing day after day with an open heart and open ears. I prayed every day and asked God what I should do. He instructed me to throw my net on the other side of the same boat, and I eventually received a new position that allowed a more stable schedule to fulfill my duties as a mother and work on my purpose. My obedience began with my ability to be able to hear God's voice. Yeshua left us with a guide, and He is the Holy Spirit. To hear Him means you spend time with Him. Let not your troubles harden your heart in any circumstances. Seek the kingdom and God and He will provide instruction and revelation to you that the flesh cannot see.

3. What is a miracle:

Why is this called miraculous? A miracle defined is a surprising and welcomed event that cannot be explained by natural or scientific laws and is therefore considered to be the work of a divine agency. If the disciples were fishing on one side of the boat, and I can imagine the boat was moving slightly, why were they unsuccessful in catching the fish? Why is it that after they were able to hear, adapt, and were obedient to turn around and throw the net to the opposite side that they were able to catch the abundance that was spoken of on their journey? As I grew in my position things were revealed to me as I matured. I received instructions from my Lord of how to speak, conduct myself, and when to leave an organization. Why now? God is a God of order. He reveals things in due season, when we reach a level of maturity to obtain, understand, and adapt.

If you feel you are stuck and need a divine intervention or event, open your heart and mind and listen for God's voice. Ask Him to intervene. BE FOREWARNED, though. Because God is a just God and a good, good Father, He will correct you. What does that mean? Many times, we are on the boat and Yeshua tells us to cast our net, but due to our pride and hardened hearts, we tell Him, through our actions, "I got this." Many times, God tells us to leave a company, but due to our pensions, 401(k), vacation days, and networking within that organization, we will remain spiritually void. God desires an abundance for our lives. If He tells you to let go of the comfort of your position and trust His direction, be at peace with uncertainty and filled with confidence in your faith that He will do a greater work in your life! Is it easy to be faithful when you have so many responsibilities? Of course not. But ask God to help your unbelief.

When I was with the organization that I mentioned before, after God gave me a new position, He told me to start prepping my resume to move on in six months. I thought, "Huh? Is this for real? Surely this is Satan. Why would my Father put me in this comfortable situation to then tell me to walk away? The voice that I had grown so familiar with no longer had my confidence. I told God to give me more time. Soon enough, all hell broke loose on the job. I began to get reprimanded for the skills that were once praised. I began to lose key specialists on my teams, which made my job very trying. I then experienced two years of constant transition of power with no leadership or guidance. During that time, I felt God was not speaking to me, and I could not understand why this was happening. I cried out to God, and the Holy Spirit reminded me in a dream of the date God gave me to leave one and a half years prior to experiencing this disconnection. I started going through my first trial the next week after the date of my instructed departure.

I was eventually laid off this position and I felt free. Not one second did I look to God and ask why He allowed me to get laid off. Not one breath of fear of what was next. I felt redeemed. You see, I cried out to God to redeem me, to give me a chance to show my love, faith, and confidence in Him. When I was let go, God provided an abundance of fish in community, food, finances, and everything that we needed to survive and thrive. During my time of unemployment, I was able to pay off debt, focus on my gifting, rebrand my business, and be there for my son when he needed me the most. Many people looked at me with pity, but I kept my eye on Yeshua and thanked Him for the right side of the boat. I thanked Him for what may have appeared to be lack to many, but was an abundance that I needed time to haul in.

Last point on this lesson. When the disciples hauled the fish on the boat, Jesus told them to bring the fish to Him. Do not forget where your abundance comes from. Take it back to Him and ask Him what you need to do with your blessings. Pay your tithes, be a blessing, be a difference! Never think it is all about you. Let Him use you to be a driving force to those around you!

4. Fishing in the water with immature fish

When we cast our rod and started getting nibbles from the baby fish, also known as fry, I was instructed that we needed to move around the pond to locate the more mature fish. That was our goal—to catch an older bluegill. While we were there, we already had a comfortable spot in the shade when the fry came. I did not want to move to the area where the mature fish were because it was in the sun; it was uncomfortable and would leave me with a nasty tan.

This reminds me of the scripture in Matthew 7:6: "Do not give dogs what is holy, and do not throw your pearls before pigs, lest they trample them underfoot and turn to attack you." How do pearls, swine, fishing, and corporations relate? In this context, Jesus was speaking of wisdom and what is holy. He instructed us not to throw what is holy to uncaring men and women, but to find fertile ground that would accept the seed and be open to hearing the truth. If you do not, and you throw your wisdom and gifting to those who are unclean, such as swine, they can eventually become contaminated, hated, and attacked. Such as by the fry. I could not catch them because of their small size and my methods of fishing. But also, they were not my intended target. Many times, in life, because of lack of understanding and no strategy, we enter circumstances unprepared, unaware, and ill-informed. The Holy Spirit and personal experience will provide revelation to us on what to do with our time and what not to do with our time. We also should be wise to listen to the instructions of those dear to us who walk in truth. If you are unsure of who these people are, pray to God for discernment.

Let us turn the page. At times, due to comfort, we let little fish trample and bite away at our bait, gifting, promises, and peace of mind. How many times have you sat in meetings and listened to professionals speak lies, cheat, steal, and attempt to ruin the lives of others? I said, "attempt to," because they only have the power to do what that individual allows. How many times have you been told that you are not enough when given instructions on how to grow? Have you been threatened to be let go from your job if you do not perform better, without a mentor present to guide you or a clear understanding of what you are even responsible for? Trust me, I have been there.

When experiencing this professional turmoil, I did not quit. I had to adjust who my target was. My target was now to exude my skill set and gifting that God had built and release it in my management style. I wanted to make Him proud, and to have an abundant return on His investment in me. I wanted to feel good and know that I was making a difference. I wanted my son to be proud that I was doing good work.

So, what did I do? After identifying my target, I moved to the other side of the pond. I started fishing for a different fish. When I started fishing for my intended target, I eventually caught something that I was not fishing for! I knew I was not supposed to catch it, but it made me proud. When I was instructed to put it back, it made me upset. Now, as a professional, I understand the sentiment. I had caught a fish too big, and, while flattering, the truth was that I was not yet prepared for it. If that were to happen to me today, I would develop a relationship with the unintended target, maybe revisit it after I mature and develop a strategy, logistics, and an operation that can support that target audience. Focus is important when you have a strategy in place—do not jump around because something else is more appealing. Trust God, trust in your ability, and trust the journey. You will get there in due time. The beauty in this is that, when you are ready, the catch will be abundant and you will be able to haul it all in with your net alone. That is why you need to continue to grow your "net" work and it will increase your "net" worth. You caught that? Very good.

Cannot Catch the Bus
at the House

"I never liked school, and your mother always got kicked out of class for running her mouth. So, I have no idea where you all got your love for school from. You are peculiar kids."

"Really, Daddy, stop calling us weird." I laughed. "You were a good student."

"I had to be. Do you know who my mother is?"

It was a reoccurring conversation at our house. My siblings and I never struggled with schoolwork, but we were very antisocial to outsiders. Well, everyone except for my brother. Everyone loved him. But to be fair, and do not tell him I said this, I thought he was weird for how he acted around his friends. He was trying too hard and watching girls all the time. They were watching him, too, but I just did not get what the fuss was about. He was a knucklehead.

Anyways. We would do what was necessary to get good grades, so we did not have to hear our parents' complaints regarding school. All of us were in honors programs or graduated with honors in academics. Some more so than others—I probably was the least interested in schoolwork out of the bunch. I just wanted to hang out in the weight room and have a fun time.

Where I grew up, there were a lot of kids in the neighborhood and all the families knew each other. My family did not have the most money, but one thing we did have was curiosity, structure, and discipline.

I can remember the days when my oldest sister decided that she was done living the rough life in the streets. The life of bike races, hide-and-seek, and climbing trees was no longer of interest to her. She was also done with doing the time for crimes she did not commit. Our days were full of adventures, but it usually ended with endless questions and repercussions. She began to focus on what she loved, and that was to bake and cook. She would spend hours with my Little Lady learning southern cooking and baking. I never saw my grandmother measuring anything, but she taught my sister all the secrets.

We never knew where my brother was, but when we did see him, he was usually taking something apart—things that were supposed to stay together. Whether it was the new radio my father bought or the VCR in the family room (look that up, kids), he was in trouble for wires being exposed. I could see it in his pointy-chinned face when his brows were overly intense and the glasses began to fog. He was in it to destroy it and destroy it he did. To give him his credit, he put it back together 96 percent of the time. The other 4 percent? Well, let us just say God loves your boy. The hilarity of it all. No matter the risk, he was drawn to electronics, building, and problem solving.

My mid-sister loved an adventure, but she had to have structure and organization. It drove me nuts. She was always so intentional with her time, and always had money. At first glance, she never looked like she had money. But beneath the mattress, in her purse, in her caboodle, on the shelf was where the money resided. I never knew where the money was coming from, and we never knew how she was able to convince our parents and grandparents to spend on her when she had her own funds.

Our family consisted of people with vastly different interests and gifts all gathered under one roof. One thing I love and am grateful for about my parents is the freedom to explore those interests and the support to be successful at them. That also meant the push to be better. You would not waste time being idle. With all these interests going on, and parents working to take care of their family, there was one solution. Riding the "Big Yellow." That's right, no carpool lane for us. We had to wake up in the morning, get dressed in a one-bedroom house, get our affairs in order with money, schedules, and uniforms, and run to the bus—which only stopped once at the end of the road.

We were not the only family running to that bus. Oh no. The entire neighborhood squad rode the bus, from kindergarten to high school. Some of the kids lived closer to the destination (bus stop) and some lived farther away.

One thing about my siblings, we looked out for each other. We still do, no matter the situation. My brother would always sprint out the house while my two sisters, who were always so planned out, would always be at the stop already, waiting on the bus. Then there was me. I had a belly situation—it was very round—and short legs. I was terrified to run for the bus. What if I fell? What if they laughed at me? What if the bus pulled away while I was making a maximum effort to get there?

I calculated all the risks and, most days, decided it was best to not even try. If the bus was there before I arrived, I made the decision to hide behind the tree in our front yard and thought of a plan to tell my mother—a mother who had just returned home from a late shift nursing patients to health. She more than likely wanted to relax, shower, and unwind. Nevertheless, I made the decision that, instead of trying to run for my bus, I would tell my mother, whose feet were screaming and whose bed was surely calling her name, that I needed a ride to school. I had to leave without delay as well; I was the elementary school news anchor. I had people depending on me to bring the good news and plans for the day. I needed to get to school, just had to go a different way.

Transferrable Lessons

1. Run to Catch the Bus

There is a long way from the house to the bus stop in your mind. You know the road, the neighborhood. You know all the landmarks that you must pass to get to your destination because you are knowledgeable of the land. Every time you went on a mission before, you surveyed the land. You studied the atmosphere. Now that it is time to complete a task, it is daunting. Why is that? Why is it that when you are participating in fun activities, or social events without an intended end goal, there is no fear? But when you are completing or participating in an activity that requires focus, strategic planning, a schedule, and a concerted team effort, there is a thought of, "I may not make it, so should I even try?" In my experience, in organizations, I have often been given many tasks that first appeared as if I do not have the skill set or experience to complete them. What if I started the activity and then fell straight on my face in front of executives and stakeholders? What would they whisper to each other as I present evidence of my position and thought process? Would they see me as being the simple-minded country girl who does not have much professional experience? Or would they hear me out, understand my communication style, understand my presentation, and give me a fair shot without bias? The thing about life is, you never know how some-one will see you or judge you. The mindset of "I will fail" is a sure way to doom your chances of winning.

When I was a little girl, I allowed all the things that I disliked about myself to get in the way of me even trying to catch the bus. My stomach was too big, my legs were too short, my hair would curl back up if I started sweating when I ran to catch the bus. My bookbag was too heavy because it was full of books that I enjoyed reading, my clothes were hand-me-downs, and when I ran, I was convinced everyone would see me as if in a spotlight and realize they were not new.

After I was done tearing myself down, I started to look at others and compared myself to those around me who had no issues catching the bus. "Look at her long legs and lean build—she is built to run quicker! Look at his short hair—he does not even have to worry about his hair curling up and looking crazy after sweating. Look at her fresh K-Swiss and new jeans—she is looking good. I do not have any of those things. I cannot measure up." My mindset of being in lack-of-resources mode clouded my ability to look inward at the things that I had that were more than sufficient to get me to the bus stop on time. There were many things I could control. For starters, I could be disciplined enough to prepare my uniform the night before. I could rise before my siblings who had the ability to run quicker, so I would have a head start. I could ask one of my siblings to help me carry my load of books. I could have also developed a relationship with my bus driver to allow me time to get to the bus if he saw me running.

When you have a mindset of lack, it is so easy to feel defeated before you even start. I challenge you to take an optimistic approach to challenges or new beginnings. Make a strategic approach to tackle the challenge so you can move forward with grace.

2. What is It?

What is the goal? To catch the bus. What time does the bus arrive? What time do I need to leave my house? What are my challenges in making it in time? Who are people that are experienced in catching the bus, and can they give me insight on how to make it there? Can I ask for an accountability partner to make sure I leave the house on time? What happens if I miss the bus? Who does that impact and how? What happens when I catch the bus?

What is preventing you from making it to your destination? One of the best things that has happened to me in my career is getting stuck when I was lost. To advance or win a game with little to no effort can make you feel accomplished. To advance in a field that does not line up with your goals and gifts is a life wasted. That sounds harsh, huh? When I was a little girl, I dreamed of becoming an interior designer and a lawyer. I loved colors and decorating, and because I had ample evidence that I could hold my own and win a good debate.

As I entered the talent development age, I took a test that confirmed my interest in legal practices, which was exciting, but it also made me feel as if I were leaving a part of me behind. As most teenagers do, I began to research the salary and knowledge requirements for both fields. I learned that the skillset to be an interior designer meant I needed to move far away, and I could not use my softball skills to get a scholarship to my schools of choice. So, I leaned into business. I approached college just as that little girl had approached catching the bus—I was afraid. I did not want to leave my family, my boyfriend, and what was familiar to me. I knew how to succeed—or at least, not fail—in the familiar place. Going away was something different altogether.

I went to college intending not to like it, but I did anyway. My desire not to make the most of it, though, did prevent me from networking and taking full advantage of the opportunities, but God is merciful and I was allotted an opportunity for an internship in Portland, Oregon, on the West Coast. Still afraid of failure, I went to the internship with one foot in the door of opportunity and one foot still holding onto the familiar.

During the internship, I had a brunch with one of my mentors. It was a nice lunch; there was a parade in downtown Portland and we enjoyed French toast. She looked at me and asked me, "Will you stay if presented with the opportunity?" I was so naïve, I responded out of emotion and not out of strategy or discipline. I stated, "I love it here, but I don't know if I can move this far away from my family. They need me." She looked at me and smiled and told me of her journey traveling the world, but also having the opportunity to visit home as much as she liked.

It was an insightful brunch, and I never forgot her words of encouragement to me. When the internship ended, my manager called me in his office for my assessment. He told me I was a curious and bright young lady. He enjoyed working with me, and although my assignment was new to me, that he was encouraged by my engagement and determination. He did tell me they would not be offering me a job at that time, but he wanted me to stay connected so that when I had more experience in the industry, I could apply and use him as a resource.

At the time of receiving my feedback, I did not think much about how the brunch, my mindset, and my assessment correlated. Five years later, it became so clear. I was naïve in how organizations operated and intertwined. I did not understand the extent that a company would take to vet and really understand a candidate they would be potentially investing in. It took five years for God to reveal to me the door that was open and that I walked away from because I was afraid to run and catch the bus to something new.

In the decade following that internship, I did have another job, and I did meet amazing people, but I never was able to match the blessing that God gave me. The internship was allowed only to athletes. I played softball for seventeen years. My scholarship, academic honors, and connections with my university paved the way for me. My talents created an avenue for me to be great, and I turned it down because of my fear of failure. I share this intimate experience in my life in hopes that I encourage someone to run. Run away from fear. Run, and if you fall, get back up and keep running. Run without worrying if you measure up because you are beautifully and wonderfully made. Run without comparison to those running with you—they are running their own race. Prepare for the run or be strategic enough that you can walk to the bus stop before the bus arrives, with enough time to connect with those who are waiting to take the journey of chance along with you.

Black Book: Big Rube

As my mother drove her Chevrolet Celebrity past the trees and a warehouse plant, the roads began to get shorter, and the houses felt closer together. After we traveled fifteen minutes, we pulled into my maternal grandmother's yard, who we called Big Rube. Her large yard with a white house and money-green shutters is in the city limits of our small town. My mother put the car in park and would sit in the car to chat with her mother through the window. If she turned off the car, we knew we were staying for a minute. Whenever we visited her, we would usually go inside the house if she had a lot going on.

My grandfather usually would be leaning on the neighboring fence, laughing with his longtime friend. The conversations would sound like a dispute, but if you listened closely, it was barbershop talk and them taking jabs at each other. Sometimes I would watch him laugh with his friend just to see if his friend would drive off on the lawn mower that he was always sitting on. They were a fun pair. After my grandfather would finish his conversation, he would sometimes come to the door and loudly say, "Rube, I'll be back!" and then off to the store he went. He was so tall that he would not come on the steps and still be able to open the door to let her know he was leaving.

My grandfather and grandmother's dynamic were well balanced. My grandmother is the sweetest person I will ever meet. She always offers a home-cooked meal whenever you come over. Whether it is in the middle of the day, or late at night, she is ready to cook. One thing about my grandmother, though—she is always working on something. In her hand, she keeps a black book. At that point, I never asked questions, and I never looked in her book, but it was there.

I remember people leaving their children at her home for her to watch and she would of course say yes. She has always stated that children make her stay young. If you ask her today how old she is, she will tell you sixteen years old. Sometimes, because Rube would always say yes to help people, those same people would stop asking permission. They began to expect it. That is when my grandfather balanced her sweetness. He would tell you like it is. He was not afraid to say no. He was not going to let you take advantage of his sweetheart. Sometimes, he would say it so rough, I could hear my grandmother in the kitchen yell, "Jesus, Monk!" "Monk" was his nickname.

My siblings and I would laugh in the guest room because we were not allowed to be in "grown folks' business." At Rube's house, it was an open door. Anyone was welcome to come sit down. When you walked in her house, you could feel the peace permeate through the walls. My grandparents' life together was not easy, but they made it easy by having a code for how they operated. They understood each other, what was allowed in their home, and my grandfather made sure that Rube's kindness did not interrupt that. There was an upspoken schedule of lunchtime and dinnertime. Westerns had an hour on the television, and soap operas had its three hours. During baseball season, so did the Atlanta Braves. If you could help it, you would not want to invite them to a cookout or family gathering during game time. They would leave you.

My grandmother has what seems like a million grands and great-grands. Some by blood and some borrowed. She welcomes you with a smile and she does not talk much. But she listens. Her husband did all the talking. One thing about Rube—under that smile, she was thinking about business, her money, and her black book. See, she was a mother of five and a nurse, which came with great responsibility. A lot of experiences helped shaped my grandmother into who she is today.

One thing that has taught me a great deal is her ability to maintain a home, her business, and her money and remain sweet. My grandmother and grandfather had a history of love and, of course, not-so-good stories. Listen, if you need good love stories, read the Bible or talk to your grandparents. The thing I love most about my grandparents is that they were so opposite in personality but shared the same moral code. Outspoken and always ready, my grandfather would chase you with his rifle if you came at him wrong, whereas my grandmother will smile at you and feed you and tell you to take a nap if you seem stressed. They constantly checked each other and did so with grace. It was off the table to be safe and dishonest with each other. It was off the table to let the other person get taken advantage of. It was off the table to allow someone to come into their home and interrupt their system, their peace.

One day, I finally got the courage to ask her what was in that black book.

She smiled at me and asked, "What black book?"

I said, "The book that you are always writing in. The small one."

She smiled again and said, "This book has all the names of people I need to remember in it. It has their address, their phone number, and how much money they owe me." We both laughed, but then she said, "Whew Jesus!" So, I knew she was telling the truth.

"So, do you keep a record of everything, or just big things?" I asked.

She responded, "What is big? It is always big, especially when you cannot remember what it is. I keep track of my money."

"Interesting," I thought. Here I see this woman being nice to everyone, and then when they leave her presence she is writing in that book. It now had me wondering. Did they owe her money or were they just a name to remember? How did she determine who should be remembered and who she should lend money to? Why did she just start writing down all this information?

The day that my grandfather decided to return to heaven, I just knew my grandmother would fall apart. But she did not. She was hurt, yes. She grieved, yes. But after more than half a century with my grandfather, my grandmother took the loss with grace, with understanding, and like a boss. From the outside looking in, I saw my grandmother adjust and continue to handle her business.

It dawned on me when I got older. If I do not start writing things down, not only am I just spending money, but I am forgetting to spend money on my bills in time. Not only am I signing my son up for events to keep him busy, but I am also wearing myself out by forgetting the time and not having things lined up to enjoy the event.

If I do not keep a written record of things at work, handling my business, how can I manage a team? When leading projects, working with vendors, managing auctions, how can I remember what happened and who owes me money? When managing associates, how can I provide feedback on performance and capitalize on teachable moments if events are not notated?

Here my grandmother is, running her business, and family members, including myself, just saw her as this lady that was just sweet and had an open door. No, she is everything a woman in business studies to become. She kept inventory of food supplies to feed her babies and company. She was a finance manager when tracking her invoices, accounts receivables, and payables. She was a project manager raising her five children, keeping the house clean, attending church, and being on the kitchen committee to feed other families. She was an executive assistant, a loving wife and mother.

My Rube taught me how to keep pushing, use what you have and manage it, in my little black book.

Transferable Lessons

1. What is big?

The power of perspective. Psychologically, is it easier to prepare yourself for larger and tougher challenges and to dismiss smaller ones as easy and give it less energy? Before coming into the revelation that all things are equal, I would gauge my challenge and subconsciously decide how much energy and prep time I would put into an ordeal. I was using this approach in my personal and professional life when it came to handling business and completing tasks. In my upbringing and within the organization, when I have a larger responsibility or managing a project with a higher valuated risk, I will block planning time on my calendar, intentionally separate myself from all distractions, and document a strategy from evaluation, resources, to implementation structure and discharge of functions. Do I have it all figured out at that time? Do I know everything that is needed? No. But it is always good for me to have a rough draft.

That day with Rube, she challenged my thought process. What is big? What determines in my mind what is important enough for a strategic plan as opposed to a shooting-the-breeze approach? As I received promotions in the organization, I learned that smaller projects sometimes had the most immediate impact on the organization and value added to the customer's experience. Why would I not take the time to see it through just as thoroughly and partner with peers to get a second eye on what I was working on? Rube taught me to approach each project the same. Create an outline and expand based on the risk, time, and resources needed to complete the project on schedule. No project management school, no million-dollar experiment. She taught me that if I could manage what I have on a small scale, then I could manage things on a larger scale, too. Create the outline, execute.

2. Do they owe her money or were they a name to remember?

This was the most amazing lesson that I learned from Rube. I am not the woman who will remember your name, your birthday, or where I know you from. It is nothing personal; it is just not my gift. My mother would always go down the list of her siblings, my father, and my siblings before finally getting to my name when she was calling me. I used to laugh, yet here I am. The same person. When I watched my grandmother manage her black book and made note of who owed her money, it amazed me. Not because she was generous, but because she documented everything. One lesson you learn in the South—do not lend money that you cannot afford to live without. That is because, well, people do not pay you back. Not that it is okay not to get paid back, but it is not financially responsible for you to give before your cup is full. Nonetheless, the point is, remember people's names that you are doing business with. Not only do you remember their name, but you also remember their dog's name, their spouse's name, children of course, and what is important to them.

Why is that important? Well, when you make people a priority to you, more times than not, they will respect you and feel connected to you. When that is the case, see them as an ally. Not necessarily as a friend, but someone that you cannot partner with as a viable resource in the organization. Now remember, you cannot do everything on your own, so it is imperative that you connect with people, build relationships with them, and then thrive with and through those relationships. This can be positive and negative. When you are connected to people in the organization who are not seen in a positive way, that can also dim your light and affect your brand. One old saying that birds of a feather flock together is still something that supervisors and authoritative figures consider when running an organization.

Be strategic with who you connect with, who you mentor, who you allow to mentor you, and who you go to lunch with within a workplace. Do they owe you money, or are they a name to remember? Are they someone to connect with that can enhance your experience or advance your mission in the organization? *Disclaimer: By no means am I encouraging you to use any individual for the selfish reason of abusing their gifting for your insecurities. I am encouraging you to develop healthy and positive relationships where you can both pull people closer to their gifting and God's design for their life. Do not get caught up with minions and distractors.

Pot Plant Christmas

My parents would not complain—well, not to us—but they would always have talks. They were always working on something. Money, the yard, the house, they were like ants. We grew up on a lot with a home that was approximately one thousand square feet. We are a family of six, and my brother was the only person to have his own room, because we were not that country. As we got older, I eventually outgrew the ability to share our small room with my two older sisters, so at night, I would pull a bed cart out to sleep in the living room. As a child, though, I did not even mind. Somehow, I knew this was temporary. My parents were the youngest parents in the community and at the church, and they did what they needed to do to ensure we had what we needed. That meant we did not have the newest of everything, and I remember the hand-me-down conversations I had with my mid-sister when it was trading day.

Every Christmas, my father would take us to a tree farm to pick our Christmas tree. No matter how hard times were, there was something special about the smell of pine during the winter. He would stop working to help us decorate the tree and put lights on the porch. It was a special time for us. We also got dressed up in the evenings to enjoy or participate in the church

Christmas programs. There was so much pie and cake. Yes, I have a sweet problem. I am okay with my flaws and waistline.

There was one Christmas when I realized that we did not have a tree, and it was within two weeks of the special day. I approached my father about it, and he said, "Maybe not this year."

I did not know what he had going on, but I knew I was going to have a tree and decorations. I waited until my parents were at work and snuck into the attic to pull down the lights and ribbons that we stored away the year prior. After I had the decorations laid out, I went in the yard to find my tree. Well, it was winter, and everything was dead. As I was returning into the warm house feeling defeated, I saw a house plant in the corner. The plant was well on its way to see Jesus, but I had faith in my decorating abilities to make it look alive again. I picked the pot plant up and placed it under the window where the tree would go. I decorated that plant for the angels and tied a blanket around the pot to resemble the tree skirt.

After I was satisfied, I left the house riding my bike, no longer thinking about it. I rode my bike in the neighborhood enjoying my friends and the conversations about what we would get for Christmas.

When my father and mother got home, and saw the makeshift tree, as if by magic, an artificial tree appeared soon after. I did not understand how that happened, but my brother kept laughing and mentioning something about a Charlie Brown tree.

After that year, I started paying attention to money and material things. I noticed that I did not have the newest of anything and that the people around us reminded us of that. We were teased on the bus and at church events. I did not let it bother me because I felt it did not matter or change who I was. We also knew, somehow, that it was temporary. We knew God had us.

One day, when I was in the yard playing, my grandfather came by on the tractor and told me to jump on. I did not ask questions; I just got on. As we were going down the street, my grandfather made a sharp turn and started driving into the trees. "Oh my goodness! This man finally lost it!" I yelled. He laughed but kept driving. He kept ramming into trees, uprooting whatever was in his way. About an hour later, or at least it felt like an hour, he said we should head back home. He turned the tractor around and we headed back to the house. As soon as he started to press the brakes, I jumped off! I ran to my mother who was on the porch talking on the phone. I said, "Granddaddy lost it!"

She looked at me and said, "Oh yeah?"

"Um, yes!"

"You remember the dream that I had? Oh, never mind. I had a dream years ago about my house. It was a house with many windows, bricks, on land. Well, we are building a house, and it is big enough to fit all of us!" She was so happy, and she started praying and praising on the spot. All I heard was that we were moving, and I did not know how to let go. As the house building process began, the talk around the old country roads was that my father was a drug dealer. People produced all kinds of stories speculating how this was happening.

The process of building the home revealed many things to me. One thing it taught me is that people will box you in your beginnings and attempt to shame you if you try to step outside of the box they made for you. Many people saw my family in our state of "figuring it out and growing."

We had more visits than we had ever had during the building process. People came to "see" what was going on—the same people who talked about our lack of new clothes, how our hair looked, and countless other things. To be fair, looking back, our hair was dry, but no one laughing offered a drop of moisturizer.

People continued to come by and walk through the home. A home is supposed to be our sanctuary, but my parents never turned them away. The entire time, they gave God the glory. My parents are by no means pushovers, but they let everyone see. It was amazing to me, the things I heard from people's mouths. It amazed me the box that we were put in through judgment of our beginnings. They did not see the saving of money, the lack of going on family trips, the working without ceasing. They did not see the tithing and unbreakable faith, the spiritual warfare and uncompromising moral code. During this long season of seed planting, all they saw was dirt.

Transferrable Lessons

1. Old man lost it—driving in the woods:

   When my grandfather drove into the woods, I really thought he would lost it. What I did not see was my father, who was the driving force behind it all and who took a chance, planned, and started knocking down trees. Let us dissect this. Taking a chance is calculated? All that time, as a creative person who loved decorating, I would have a thought, find my tools, and go at it. I never thought that having an idea required a plan. My mother received the dream of her home years before it came to the day to knock down trees and clear the land. Why did it take so long to get started? Resources and a plan were being built and it is okay for a plan creation to take longer to shape than the timeline to complete the project. Why is that?

   Because my father was a contractor, he owned all responsibility of building, approving plans, budgets, hiring subcontractors, and keeping up with the weather and timeline. Money was on the line every day that he was off the schedule. My father not only had to work, but he had to project manage the building of his home and execute his areas of responsibility.

   Fast forward to today. I am a business owner. When creating my first home décor line, I had an idea. I knew how to file government paperwork and I had a small budget. I put no research into said budget; I had no timeline from filing to opening. I just ran my tractor off the road. That business was open, I paid taxes, and I never sold one product. My prototypes are in storage still and it was a bust. It took me a while to get over the emotions around that and figure out what I did wrong.

I have heard many people preach to take a chance on yourself. Love yourself enough to try. Jump without a plan b!!! But we never hear the emphasis on plan A. Recollecting on my experience of my parents going against all the odds and clearing land is, as an adult, walking in the revelation of the odds that were truly against them. The adversity to get a loan. The difficulty they faced with people not executing the contract. They also executed precisely on the overall timeline, and they were able to expand on the plan with a sound foundation. Why? They took the time to create a strategic plan. They wrote out their timeline, resources, vendors; common and strategic partnerships and executed.

After considering my environmental experiences, I dissolved my business and planned before I started again. I asked God to help me with my hand in the business. Provide me with business acumen, wisdom in this industry, and the drive to not give up. In the first month of business, I sold ten more units than my plan called for, and I have been planning for expansion ever since. Plan for the risk that you are taking. Never jump without a clear evaluation of where you stand today and where you want to exist in the near and far future.

My last transferrable lesson can only be so clear. Throughout my life, I always felt so connected to nature. I could listen to the trees dance, the dogs prance, and the wind turn the chimes. I would listen to the bikes racing, the rakes moving, the lawn mower creating a sweet aroma of grass. I could see the smoke rise from the leaf piles and then turn to ashes in the fall. I would watch the neighbors laugh and the flowers bloom and the grapevine burst in harvest. I watched the tadpoles swim, the earthworms hide, and the pecans hit the gravel. I watched the ducks waddle, the chickens chase, and the cats climb the trees. I heard the saws cut, the nails enter, and smelled the woodchips turn dust. I watched seasons change, smelled rain coming, and watched birds to plan my action. I listened to elders live and watched siblings grow and find their purpose through trial.

I grew up in a small town in South Carolina, where it was sweet to just be. Then I became an adult and moved to a city where people rushed around to succeed. Along the way, I lost sight of the lessons that university never taught me. But the sweet breeze in the country wrapped my being in lessons and experience. Never dismiss your beginnings and your experiences. They can never be removed from you. Never allow people to brand you and tell you who you will become because your story is different from theirs. Remember, God made you in His image, and He said His creation was good. No one can stop you from flying high; no can stop you from being free. You must remain anchored and have pure intent. Use your journey to impact the lives that are intertwined with yours from this day forward, in light.